About the Author

Amy Tollyfield has performed her poetry at Clifton Literature Festival, The Wardrobe Theatre (Bristol), The Barbican Theatre (Plymouth), Waterstones (Clifton, Bristol), Foyles bookstore (Bristol), and The Loco Klub (Bristol), among other venues and events. She has a Master's degree in Shakespeare Studies (Birmingham), a Bachelor of Arts (Hons) degree in Drama and Theatre Practice (Hull) and is a former registered member of the National Youth Theatre.

Toy Soldiers is Amy's second collection of poetry. Her first, *The Suicide*, was published by Olympia Publishers in 2018.

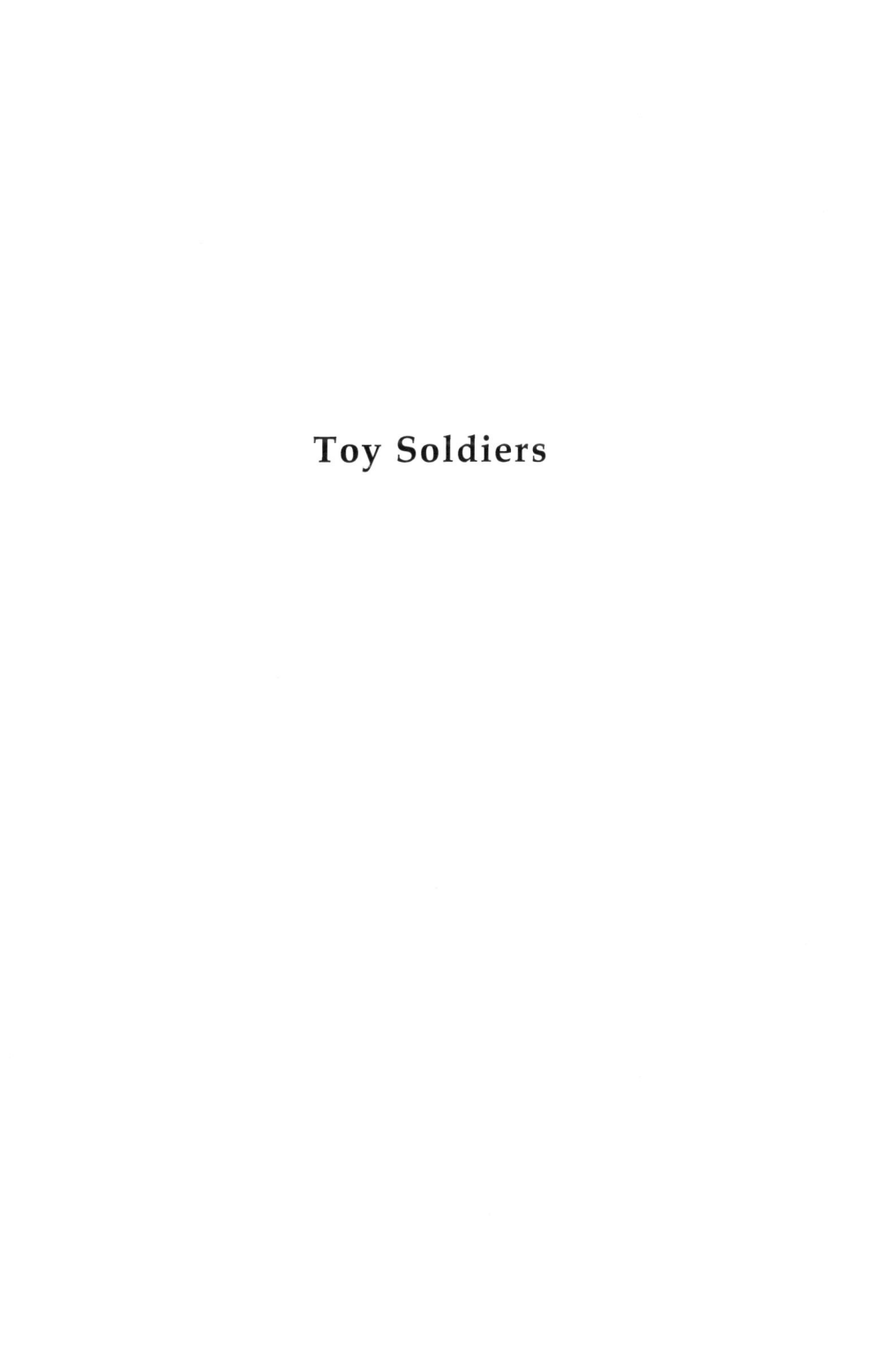

Toy Soldiers

Amy Tollyfield

Toy Soldiers

Olympia Publishers
London

www.olympiapublishers.com
OLYMPIA PAPERBACK EDITION

Copyright © Amy Tollyfield 2020

The right of Amy Tollyfield to be identified as author of
this work has been asserted in accordance with sections 77 and 78
of the Copyright, Designs and Patents Act 1988.

All Rights Reserved

No reproduction, copy or transmission of this publication
may be made without written permission.
No paragraph of this publication may be reproduced,
copied or transmitted save with the written permission of the
publisher, or in accordance with the provisions
of the Copyright Act 1956 (as amended).

Any person who commits any unauthorised act in relation to
this publication may be liable to criminal
prosecution and civil claims for damage.

A CIP catalogue record for this title is
available from the British Library.

ISBN: 978-1-78830-794-9

First Published in 2020

Olympia Publishers
Tallis House
2 Tallis Street
London
EC4Y 0AB

Printed in Great Britain

Dedication

To Nanny

Acknowledgments

I'd like to thank Olympia Publishers for their continued faith in me and God, in whom, on the whole, I still believe.

Amy's first collection of poetry, *The Suicide*, was published by Olympia Publishers in August 2018. Since the book's release, Amy has performed her poetry at a variety of venues and events across the south west of England, including at Clifton Literature Festival, The Barbican Theatre in Plymouth and The Wardrobe Theatre in Bristol. Amy has also given poetry readings of her work at Waterstones in Clifton and Foyles bookstore in Cabot Circus, both venues in Bristol.

Toy Soldiers

I lined them all up,
Then I heard the telegram,
Bundled them all back in their box, and sat for a while
in silence.

A few months passed
And I didn't take them out again to play with; heard in
the village that there would be a service so I put on my
Sunday best and

Took the wooden box with me. Private, gunner and
lance corporal rattling around to the sound of drums. I
waited until the adults were stood

Around a small girl reading a poem.
I took my moment to claw at the fresh earth
Some yards away, let my nails carve out a modest home
and interred my boys forever.

Plate of Peas

Meeting for dinner, I look in your eyes
Which betray you. I'm wise
To a woman's mind; I hypothesize
That you were hoping for a man twice my size.

The disappointment ebbs. You reach for your drink:
A rosé. I mumble that I think I'll have the risotto.
You barely blink
And order the salmon which arrives pink.

There's sadness in mine and a tinge of regret. 'You've a plate full of peas
That you've not finished yet. This is quite deep
And we've barely met.' I swallow hard
And take a sip to forget.

You reach for your jacket — follow the trend.
I try not to answer
(My thoughts I suspend). I reach for the door, offer it open;
I've learnt to be patient and lovingly broken.

Brickwork

I'd settle for the one-up, two-down,
The kind of brickwork that makes the neighbours frown,
To know that inside lived her sights, smells,
Her kindred passion; heaven, hells;

The shoe she threw; lit a match or two; the carpet she
lay on, the walls she knew; the fireplace; her home, her
rules;
My fiery heart and working tools.

The films she loved, watched back to back, then later
on: the beaten track,
The dog we lost, the wasted tears; a child's football;
forgotten years;

The smell of liquor, the smell of lust; the abandoned
car-park I learnt to trust; the high-heels she left long
behind — and that brickwork: the frowning kind.

Gentle Rain

Be the rainwater I have always known, the quiet cuddle, the smell of home;
The freshly baked cakes, the loving smile, the warmth and will to reconcile.

Be the fire that keeps me toasty,
The soothing voice, but darling, mostly, be the rock on which I may build
A bed of dreams, a life fulfilled.

You are my spring, my Easter egg,
I want to unwrap you: feel your body instead. I can be tender, I can be soft,
Just promise to care and to think of me oft.

The twilight beckons, the wilderness ends,
I forget sorrows and feel the warmth of my friends.
The cracks are healed over, the dawn breaks anew, and under the canopy, still smiling, is you.

Ring

I lost a ring.
I don't know where I put it — seem to always lose these things; don't know why I got it.

I checked behind the sink; found a silver band for sure, put my finger in its pockets (not unlike the one I wore).

But it was not my baby,
And it did not know my name.
I think my ring has found another and I should do the same.

Sometimes we choose to falter; buy the gold of lesser worth.
I dare not buy the diamond lest I lose it from my purse.

Apocalypse

I did not know that the fire could lick deep to the heart of the city-in-sick.

I dance on my heels to the sirens sounding; faith to the floor and my heartbeat pounding.

I did not know that you'd found a way out: quiet in the home after this roundabout.

I find you alone in our marriage bed;

I shut out the noise and I love you instead.

Red Skies

It was not lingering; it was just brief;
The light-fingered work of a vagabond thief.

It did not penetrate; it was not deep;
Less thorough and meaningful than a cheap chimney-sweep.

And yet I remember the pockets of hurt
That your touch drifted over as I showed you my worth.

I wanted for nothing; to only resent;
But the less it was poignant, the more that it meant.

Patience

A broken fence; an open door; you enter in
For something more.

A lady's touch;
A welcome face;
The scent of longing, a warm embrace.

But none of this will you find there.
You're better waiting anywhere.

Patience is
The kindest grace:
She will find you
Some time, some place.

Boudicca

Her daughters write the history, ravished as they were.
A blot of ink and then no more — a testament to her.

'Rise up, rise up, my fellow men,' she bellowed in the heat.
With scarce a chance to catch our breath, we stumbled to our feet.

We beat down doors along the way, and killed the Roman scum.
Set fire to the ivory
And thought the battle won.

Imperialism overthrown, we settled down to tea. Neither Anglo, nor of blood from lands across the sea.

But this was just the start of it, and little did we know,
The Romans at the heart of it thought smarter than their foe.

They crept inside within the night, and took us as we

slept.
Swifter than a swallow's flight; in victory, adept.

Boudicca, we lost in arms; she took herself away.
Some say she drowned of misery, others say one day

Boudicca might come again, her daughters held aloft.
A stone in place of that which beats and keeps a woman soft.

Nina

In my mind, we meet again,
Backs to the wall like the oldest of friends. You'd wear Ralph Lauren,
Me in Chanel.
You'd sheepishly ask me if I have been well.

I'd nod in reply
And ask you the same.
You'd say you're tired of the niceties game. 'Have the years been kind?'
The words cut me deep.
I firmly but fairly bid you go back to sleep.

But your vision won't blur or disappear.
Your hand reaches over but I don't come near. I pray and I plead
For your ghost to leave,
And slowly but surely, I feel the reprieve

As your image begins to fade to the wall,
I'm left with your scent or nothing at all.
Some things are better to never know.
One last breath of perfume then I let you go.

Horse d'Oeuvres

I remember the details because I loved you.
But it was not the storybook kind of love that you were
hoping for. No hand-holding or kisses in the dark;
Just missed calls and wanting to know where you were.

In the heavy shadows at night, my body moved toward
your own; an arm gripped you, a mouth searched for
you.
A restless sigh heaved itself into the air, and we fell
back to sleep, entwined.

At your brother's wedding, we stole glances, met each
other in the bathroom.
I undid your corset; you yielded, willingly,
As the other guests boasted and whinnied over hors
d'oeuvres.

I've lost you, now: the horse lost its gallop; ran through
fences, fields and ravines, chased through barley,
gasped for air;
And neighed, neighed, collapsing. Thinking, breathing,
feeling — almost gone save opening its eyes and
sighing, 'once you were mine, once you were mine,
once you were mine.'

Cradle

'I wish I'd never met you,' she sighed.
Her elbows at least three inches deep,
And her arms at right angles.

I flicked to a different page.
The first was the outbreak of war, the second,
The high-street collapse.

She pushed the spoon away one last time,
Closed the newspaper shut and watched me with
caution.

I said, 'hush, hush.
'Didn't we hurt each other enough?' I made my feet into
a bowl,
My legs a cradle.

Pebble

Skipping across water to some unknown home, the
pebble dances as nature begins.
Breathing in time with my whispers alone, the trembling
leaves give way to the winds.

A short mile away, an office-worker clicks
On a mouse, bringing a computer to life.
A waitress speeds to a table to fix
The layout: the napkin was missing a knife.

A hospital bed welcomes in a new child; the woman
who bore him crying in relief.
Next door, an old man, once youthful and wild, says his
goodbyes and enters the peace.

The moors have seen life in dutiful motion — their
tender waters licking anew.
The pebble drops to the depths of the ocean and dances
again with the bottomless blue.

Build Me a Nest

Settle me down so I may show you

The darkest of recesses, the chalice of blue.

Write me a symphony that I may hold
Your heart in the small of me; a current of gold.

Show me the nothing that you keep discreet
That I may make copies of the things you will keep.

Send me to somewhere where I may find rest;
I'm cold and I'm hurting so build me a nest.

Lemongrass

I broke into lemongrass; it was quite clear.
You showed me an opening so I could draw near.

We eloped in sweet memories: they'd glittered the stage.
I kept you on tenterhooks until the last page.

Somewhere there's a melody you and I danced to.
I've forgotten the words and you've not had the chance to

Write back to me with how things are going. The lemongrass wilted now winter is snowing.

Brighter Stars

Hatstand memories,

And a loveless bride dances the aisles
(She's mine inside).

Buttercup;
Did you mean to love a clearer mind?
(She's mine on top).

Pace the halls because I'm the one
Who's building an empire, who's barely begun.

You think you know her; better yet:
Choose brighter stars you can forget.

Lover

The drops
Fall like little magnets
And I watch where you are standing.

Handcuffs
And pillow-talk
Has never been quite enough.

The serene air whispers candidly
From the corners of the landing.

I breathe and I sleep
And I hope we're strong enough.

Wind

What happened to the time? The way whispers move.
The drop of your patience. The slight of your love.

I fret for the sunshine; I fret for the breeze.
You clasp an island: I want for the seas.

Over the years, my body groans
For tears and for safety
And to know female moans.

The clock is still ticking — the dawn yet begins —
But you know that to love me is to lean on the wind.

Mirror

I look into the mirror and a million ghosts
Are saying 'hold her close', but I don't know how.

She comes to me from the dark places.
The places I never knew 'tween old
And new.

I've a softer hand; maybe
In the future
I could meet demand.

For now, I rest
'Tween dreams I have
And what is best.

Weston

Violet skies under which you parted lips
To show me a deeper truth.

I watched vagabonds and devils
Stand inside
Your bitter memories.

Sea breeze, fresh beaches;
You hold my hand to centre me.

The repercussions are stark; I'm left untame.
Swirling winds whisper your name.

Undone

We are not as we think we are, though undone:
The colder morning leaves footprints for the sun.

I held you close,
Though ice would prove a better friend;
Made tea and toast in hope that I could make amends.

There is a brook —
Runs silent through the frosty nook;

I took you there,
In hope that I could maybe share a simpler time,
A love you'd know until you've mine.

The sun goes in — the shadows cast a longer smile (we can look in).

I bear some hope,
Though most in truth was washed away within the brook:

I would have loved, but all I took.

Clean Sheets

Somewhere
Under stacks of bric-a-brac lies a bed made,
Its sheets clean on top.

Once it was dishevelled; made hardy through
Tears of longing and some of rejoice, and female moans
dancing in the air.

One time you stayed there, told me not to call again but
that you'd remember me a few years down the line.

I hadn't the balls
To pick up the phone when you rang. Hoped that
memory would satisfy, and lay down on clean sheets.

At the Font

Perfectly viable, written in stone,
To alter and falter when being alone.
The averageness wilters on knowing all else;
A half-hearted duty between a lost sense of self.

Did you write diamonds on resting the pen? A silent
watchman stands bewildering, then, you open it up, just
to wish you had not,
Remembering a silence which you'd hoped you'd
forgot.

They talk of the spring and of opening hearts, but I'm
closed off in my various parts; favouring nothing to
everything raw,
And settling pennies just to lower the score.

You can make promises, love if you want, but I rest in
knowing I could lay at the font,
Progress and forwardness building their homes, as I
savour the tenderness of being alone.

The Victoria Line

Dark and brooding,
I am of ominous matter, caught somewhere between
The Victoria Line
And the better days you had when I was free.

I'd watched birds cry out in the morning
(I don't know their names — how could I?)
With their hopeful morning song, to welcome in my
memories.

I sit in that forgotten carriage, shunting about,
With my bags packed,
Looking around at all of the faces (I used to practice
empathy)
But none of the eyes meet mine.

You push my head to your shoulder, kiss the scalp,
Mere bones breathing in the polluted air;
I'm glad we can survive together.

Leather

If I come back
(And I may never come back), may I be warm to the touch and tender;
Shacked up in a terraced that's slender, with a girl and a babe and a blender.

May I watch rom-coms in the winter; polish boots 'til the leather might splinter —
Shop for nuance and style in the cereal aisle and make love in the ways that we think ter'.

I've got marks on my arm — they're on purpose; paid a gent to make art in my surface.
Carved an angel in snow just to learn to let go; met her eyes as they searched for a reason.

Show the workings to me in the heathen; I won't believe you 'til baby is breathing.
Roaring fire and a stove, and a heart, I suppose, and a pain I can trust in all seasons.

P's and Q's

I'm told that (as a woman)
I should mind my p's and q's.

And I do
But I swear
Like a trooper.

I am polite but rude
And sometimes undignified.

Somewhere
In this cold earth
I belong.

Waterfalls

Sometimes
It breaks and falls and all I'm left with are waterfalls
And all they stand for rushes down
To lava pools beneath the ground
And I stand watching
Wishing that
I hadn't been through all of that
My mind becomes an estuary
So purify
What's left of me.

Backless

If I had the chance
I would be twirling you around again, all high-heels and backless dress, with me in the tux.

You would want for nothing and I would be the giver;
Spending my time and love on you as you learnt how to care for me.

No back-tracking or second thoughts, and lie-ins on the weekend; cocktails and cheese for all of us; eyes glazed over at the ceiling,

Blood on your hands and on mine, bite-marks fresh in our necks,
Stiletto prints left in abandoned buildings, no smoke in the air.